Acknowledgements

Special thanks to the following people who gave so much of their time and help.

The members of the creche working group, Kathy Dodds, Marie Adams, Alison Wightman and Marion de Frinse, whose experience and practical common sense approach to organising creches is reflected throughout the publication.

The Field Services Sub-Committee and all members of staff who commented on the first draft/and second or contributed in any way to the development of this publication.

Sonia Longridge, Anne McMillan and Carol McNamara who proof read and edited the work in progress.

Roisin Hughes who typed and retyped with such patience.

Thank you to the 'Equality Commission for Northern Ireland' for helping with funding the reprinting of this publication.

NIPPA would like to dedicate this reprint to the memory of Marion de Frinse, who sadly died on 31st October 1999.

Cathy Lyle
NIPPA Early Years Adviser

March 1997
Reprinted 2002
2nd Edition

INTRODUCTION

Creches provide a time limited daycare option for parents/carers of young children. They are often used by adults attending educational classes or other training sessions. They can also provide parents/carers with the opportunity to engage in social/recreational activities. Being cared for in a creche is often a child's first experience of being separated from his or her parents/carers. It is therefore the responsibility of all concerned to make sure that creche provision provides a high quality experience.

NIPPA is committed to helping creches provide high quality care and education. Following a resolution passed at the 1994 Annual General Meeting requesting that NIPPA produce written guidelines for creches, a working group was formed. The aim of the NIPPA Creche Working Group has been to provide guidelines offering practical information on quality childcare within creches and a resource which may be used for staff induction and training. These guidelines should be read in conjunction with any guidelines produced by the Health and Social Services Boards/Trusts.

Statement of Principles and Values

NIPPA Values

- Early childhood in its own right as well as being the foundation for later life
- All children equally
- Play
- Parents as the first educators
- Diversity
- The central role of the adult in early childhood settings

NIPPA Promotes

- Play based, quality learning environments for all young children
- Partnership with parents and other agencies
- A co-ordinated and holistic approach to young children's learning and development
- Support for families and parents
- Equal opportunities for children and adults
- High quality ongoing training for all adults working with young children
- Increased awareness of the needs of young children and related early childhood issues

NIPPA Supports

The right of the child to protection from all forms of maltreatment, exploitation, physical, mental and sexual abuse as outlined in articles 19 and 34 of the United Nations Convention on the Rights of the Child.

Organisation
and Management

Section 1

Creches - Definition

Creches are facilities that provide occasional care for children under eight. **If they operate for more than two hours in any day they are required to be registered by Social Services under the Children (N.I.) Order 1995 whether parents are on the premises or not.**

A creche is not the same as a full daycare setting (for further information and advice on policy and practice in full daycare it is advisable that you contact the Social Worker with responsiblty for registration within your Trust area).

Wherever the word "parent" is used in this publication, it should be taken to mean parent or carer.

Creches operate in many different settings e.g.

- Education centres
- Shopping centres
- Leisure centres
- Churches and church halls

- Hospital and medical centres
- Conference centres
- Community centres
- Information centres

Creches need to be flexible to meet the different needs of parents/carers, resulting in several different types of services:

- A permanent creche providing care for a frequently changing group of children e.g. in shopping centres, women's centres, drop-in centres and for parent support groups
- A one-off creche which may be held in any venue in response to a demand for childcare
- A mobile creche where a group of creche workers use their skills to provide a service in response to demand. These workers must have the ability to adapt to different surroundings and careful planning is essential
- An occasional creche which provides care for children as and when demand arises e.g. short training courses, church and parent support groups and conferences

Administration and Effective Management Systems

Why Is It Important?

All creches should have management procedures which ensure that all the legal and constitutional requirements are met and resources are used effectively. Good management is about efficient and effective use of resources - human and financial.

Management of Creches

Voluntary and community organisations whose sole function is to provide a creche should adopt a constitution and form a management committee. NIPPA's model constitution is available to member groups. Every member of the committee should have a copy of the constitution. The constitution defines the responsibilities of the management committee and details good committee procedure.

Financing a Creche

Early in the planning process a budget should be established for both setting up and running costs. Any budget will need to include the cost of:

- Hire of premises
- Heating and light
- Toys and equipment
- Staffing - recruitment, wages/expenses
- First Aid equipment
- Changing and cleaning equipment
- Insurance and NIPPA membership
- Refreshments - for children and staff
- Training

Insurance

Creches must have public liability insurance. The policy should provide cover for the children and adults in case of an accident, protect the creche's property and equipment and should protect the creche in the event of a claim being made against it.

NIPPA offers member groups insurance cover. Full information and advice can be obtained from the Assistant Finance Officer at the NIPPA central office. If a creche is to be run for another body, such as an Adult Education or Sports Centre, check it is also covered by the centre's insurance policy. If in doubt, ask to see the policy and preferably obtain written confirmation that cover is adequate. It is essential that there is adequate insurance before the creche opens.

Administration and Effective Management Systems

Staffing Requirements

Creches usually include young babies as well as older children. To ensure that there is adequate staff cover it is important to comply with Social Services recommended staffing ratios:

I adult per 3 babies   0 - 2 years
I adult per 4 children 2 - 3 years
I adult per 8 children 3 - 12 years

In recognition of the responsible and skilled nature of work with children and to protect the rights of employees all groups should comply with fair employment legislation, groups should aim to pay staff NIPPA recommended wages for staff working in early years groups and expenses to volunteers. For more detailed information see NIPPA's Recruitment Guidelines for the Employment of Early Years Staff.

Social Services have a statutory responsibility to carry out police and health checks on all persons working with young children. This procedure applies to volunteers, casual helpers and paid staff working in a group which requires to be registered under the Children (Northern Ireland) Order 1995. It is a very confidential procedure the aim of which is to help protect children. In itself it is not a sufficient safeguard and your staff selection process should also bear in mind the need to protect children. A full child protection policy is essential and should include guidelines with regard to a code of conduct for staff.

The creche supervisor ensures that any person who has not been vetted is never left alone with the children. If a creche is provided on an occasional basis it is a good idea to keep a list of workers and volunteers who have had a police and health check carried out by social services.

Registration Form

The parent/carer of every child attending the creche should complete a registration form giving the creche staff essential information about the child and about the parent's/carer's whereabouts during the creche session.

A sample registration form is included in Appendix 1.

Register

A daily attendance register must be completed as children arrive and leave. This is essential for use in fire drills or emergencies. There should also be a procedure in place for identifying children and parents to ensure that children are collected by the correct person.

Administration and Effective Management Systems

Accident and Incident Book

An accident and incident book should be kept and the following information recorded:

- date and time of accident
- details of any accident;
- to whom it occurred;
- where it occured;
- any action taken;
- signature of adult present;
- signature of parent/carer;
- name of witness to the accident;

All accidents and incidents, no matter how minor they seem, should be noted as this can help to build up a picture of where, within the creche, accidents are most frequently occurring and at what time of day. Adjustments can then be made if required to the layout of the room and the organisation of the session.

First Aid

At least one member of staff should be trained in first aid which includes training in first aid for infants and young children and this training should be updated every three years. A first aid box must be provided which complies with the Health and Saftety (First Aid) Regulations 1981. The contents should be checked regularly and replaced as necessary by a nominated staff member. Keep out of children's reach. All adults in the creche should be familiar with its whereabouts, its contents and know the procedures for dealing with minor injuries.

Medicine

If a child requires routine medication for a specific need it should be administered by the parent. If this is not possible the following guidelines should be used:

- The creche should obtain the written consent of parents for the administration of medicine
- Medicine should be administered by the creche supervisor
- Two adults should be present when the medicine is administered
- The creche should keep a record of the administration of medicine and this should be signed by two members of staff and the parent
- Medicine must be supplied in its orginal container and with clearly written instructions

A sample administration of medication authorisation form is included in Appendix 2.

Administration and Effective Management Systems

Smoking

It is recommended that you implement a no smoking policy.

Childhood Illness

Parents and carers should be provided with information about the incubation and exclusion periods for childhood illnesses. Parents should also be informed not to bring children to the creche when suffering from vomiting or diarrhoea as these can be very contagious.

Information on childhood illnesses is included in Appendix 3.

Child Protection

There should be clearly written policies and procedures for recording, reporting and delaing with incidents of suspected child abuse and/or neglect. Creche staff should be familiar with (Volunteer Development Agency) "Our Duty to Care", and the Health and Social Services Board's Child Protection Guidelines. Child protection training should be updated annually. All staff should be familiar with procedures to follow if they suspect child abuse.

Settling In

It is important that parents/carers know what is expected of them when their child is starting the creche. They need to know that the staff would like them to stay with their child until their child is happy to stay on their own and who they should speak to when they are anxious about settling their child. Even when a child is attending a one-off creche the parent/carer should be encouraged to prepare the child for attending the creche and stay with him/her until well settled.

Staff should be told of any changes from the usual collection of children.

Information on settling children into the creche for parents and staff as included in Appendices 4 and 5.

Fire Drills

These should be held monthly, so that all children are familiar with the procedure. The time and day of the fire drill should vary and should be recorded by the creche supervisor.
Staff organising one-off creches should familiarise themselves with the fire procedures of the premises they will be using.

Administration and Effective Management Systems

Policies

It is good practice for each creche to develop written policies which describe the working procedures of the group. The following policies should be developed:

- Administering medicines and emergency treatment
- Admissions
- Child Management
- Child Protection and Adult Protection
- Complaints/Grieveance
- Confidentiality
- Equal Opportunities (staff and children)
- Healthy Eating and Lifestyle
- Induction
- Observation and Assessment
- Partnership with Parents
- Recruitment and Selection
- Reporting to Parents
- Settling-In
- Staff Development and Training

Copies of policies should be displayed and available for parents to read.

Policies should be read by new emloyees and volunteers as part of the staff induction.

For further information and checklists to help draw up policies consult NIPPA's Valuing Play, Valuing Early Childhood and Policy and Practice Guidelines for Early Years.

Legal Requirements

Registration of Creches

If you are operating, or intend to operate a creche, you should contact the local social services office to find out if the creche needs to be registered. The requirement for registration is dependent on the length of time the creche operates and the number of times per year it is open.

Criteria for Registration (Articles 118-120) Children's (Northern Ireland) Order 1995

The Order states:

Persons who provide day care for children under the age of twelve on premises (other than domestic premises) for periods exceeding two hours in any day need to register.

N.B. premises include a vehicle.

For more information on creche registration contact your local social services office.

The social worker responsible for registration will advise whether or not the premises are suitable for registration. The premises must be checked by the Fire Authority for Northern Ireland and may also be checked by the environmental health department and/or a health visitor.

Space

It is important to consider the size of the room to be used for the creche in relation to the amount of equipment and the number of adults who will be in it. The size of the room determines the number of children who can use it.

Recommended space requirements in Full Day Care Nurseries are:

Age	Square Feet	Square Meters
0-2	45	4.2
2-5	30	2.8
5-12	25	2.3

CHECKLIST FOR CRECHE PREMISES:

- Are the premises secure? ie. can you ensure the children cannot leave, or unauthorised persons enter, the premises unnoticed?
- Is there accessibility to all, including those with disability? eg. wheel chair ramp?
- Are the premises well lit and ventilated?
- Is there lots of natural light?
- Are there toilets and running water close by?
- Are there kitchen facilities close by?
- Is there a separate utility area for washing machines and tumble dryers?
- Are there adequate storage facilities?
- Are the premises clean?
- Is the heating adequate?
- Do the heaters have guards on them?
- Are radiators thermostatically controlled?
- Is the floor clean and free from splinters?
- Is there a baby changing area?
- Is there a carpeted area for babies to crawl on?
- Are there plug covers on all sockets?
- Are fire exits clearly marked?
- Are low level windows fitted with safety glass, boarding or guards?
- Are sharp corners on low level furniture padded?
- Is there the use of a telephone?
- Is the outdoor play space safely fenced off and free from rubble and glass?

Legal Requirements

Layout

As creches cater for children of varying ages the layout of the space should be organised so that children can play in groups according to their age and stage of development. Ideally there should be a room for each age group as this will allow the creation of appropriate environments for babies, toddlers and pre-school children. If the creche is limited to one room then it should be divided in a way which allows all children to play safely and happily. Dividing the room into smaller areas will create a cosier atmosphere. It is important to provide a partitioned area where babies can play and sleep in comfort.

Planning the layout of the room well before the arrival of the children gives the staff an opportunity to:

- Decide where the baby area will be positioned and what equipment will be provided
- Decide what type of play will be provided - if space is limited then it is acceptable to change some play activities as the session progresses
- Name each of these areas and inform the staff so that everyone uses the same names
- Clearly define the areas of play by labelling and partitioning with low level partitions, low storage units or equipment.

Observing children as they play enables staff to evaluate the provision and identify areas which may need changed.

It is important to be flexible in dividing the room up as the numbers and ages of children may vary on a daily basis.

HEALTHY EATING

"Learning about health is an important area of learning. If good health habits can be developed early they are likely to be continued throughout life". (NIPPA 1999)

Food for Thought:

Most creches will provide a snack and some may even provide lunch for the children. Those responsible for the preparation and handling of food must comply with regulations relating to food safety and hygiene. Alternatively, parents may be asked to send along a snack with the child. If parents are supplying food, provide an information sheet making suggestions about healthy snacks. Any parent supplying a bottle for their baby should clearly label it with the baby's name. Keep a supply of labels so that you can do this if parents forget. Babies' bottles should be kept fresh in a refrigerator. Facilities should be available for the hygienic preparation of babies feed. A record should be kept of babies food intake and shared with parents.

Provide nutritious snacks:

*   small pieces of apple or seasonal fruit
*   cubes of cheese (check for intolerancy to dairy products)
*   small pieces of raw vegetable e.g. carrot, celery, red and green pepper
*   yoghurts
*   brown, wholemeal, or white bread
*   milk

Sweets and chocolates should be avoided as should food with a high salt, sugar or fat content. Always check if children have any allergies to certain foods such as peanuts or dairy products.

Fresh drinking water should be avilable to children at all times.

Religious dietary practices and medical conditions requiring specific dietary restrictions must be taken into consideration when planning snacks.

Checklist for providing the snack/lunch

*   Who is responsible for purchasing food?
*   Agree a weekly budget for food
*   Who will prepare the food?
*   Where possible involve children in the preparation and serving of food. This helps to nurture children's independence.
*   Organisation of the break: children should preferably sit in small groups and be accompanied by an adult. This encourages good eating habits, language and social development

"An ounce of prevention is better than a pound of cure". (NIPPA 1999)

Healthy Eating

Checklist for Health and Safety

Do children wash their hands before eating food?

Do children wash their hands after using the toilet?

Do adults wash their hands before preparing food?

Do adults wash their hands after using the toilet and changing nappies?

Are disposable gloves used when changing nappies?

Are individual towels/paper towels provided for each child?

Is there a plentiful supply of tissues available?

Is there a plentiful supply of disinfectant?

Are toys/dressing up clothes regularly washed?

Is the playdough changed at least weekly?

Are all potentially dangerous products including cleaning materials and medicines stored out of reach of children in a locked cupboard?

Are tables used for food and drink cleaned before and after use?

Are individual cups/plates/dishes provided?

Are fresh fruit and vegetables washed before use?

Are tea towels kept scrupulously clean?

Is sand sieved and washed regularly?

Are dustbins inaccessible to children?

Is a first aid box provided and contents regularly checked?

Does at least one member of staff have an up to date first aid certificate? (The Leader)

The leader should ensure that all staff have a working knowledge of first aid.

Are parents issued with an information sheet specifying the conditions for attendance?

Is there a no smoking policy?

Under Two's

Are high and low chairs used with safety harnesses?

Are sleeping babies frequently checked?

Are babies held whilst feeding, preferably by the same carer?

Is suitable sterlising equipment available for babies bottles and soothers?

Are babies bottles/soothers labelled?

Are spare disposable nappies of different sizes available?

Are there adequate materials for cleaning babies during nappy changing?

Are there hygienic arrangements for the disposal of soiled nappies?

Guidelines for Developing Partnership with Parents

Parents are children's first educators and should be valued as such. The fostering of good relationships with parents must be of primary concern.

'Partnership should be a reality not just tokenism'. (Whalley 1994 page 68).

Partnerships grow through mutual understanding and respect. Parents should be made to feel welcome in the creche and need to know that their contributions and ideas are valued.

- Agree about the need to work in partnership with parents and share the creche's aims and objectives with parents
- Let parents know what creche workers expect or would like from them. Creches may wish to have parents sign a written contract. (see Appendix 6 - Sample Contract Between Creche and Parent/Carer)
- Explore different parenting styles and lifestyles and your attitudes to them
- Share information through leaflets, talks, noticeboards and magazines etc.
- Make the atmosphere welcoming and inviting. If possible, offer parents a room where they can have a coffee and a chat and access to information
- Give parents information about settling their children into the creche (see Appendix 4 - Settling Your Child into the Creche)
- Encourage parents to participate in creche activities e.g. - songs and rhymes, gathering materials for junk art etc.
- Develop a written policy on partnership with parents and involve parents in this process
- Assure parents of the groups policy on confidentiality
- Share the groups policy on confidentiality with parents
- Provide opportunities in which parents and staff can learn and train together e.g. NIPPA
- Branch meetings, parent workshops etc.
- Encourage parents to share special skills or hobbies with children in the creche
- Take time to chat informally with parents at the beginning and end of the session
- Develop a trusting and equal relationship with parents so that information can be shared about the children and their development
- Organise social events and outings
- Offer toy or book library facilities
- Encourage parents to help in fundraising activities
- Share observations of children with parents
- Share daily log of feeding/activities/toiletting/development
- Share policies

Staff Training and Qualifications

The person in charge should be qualified to NVQ III in Early Years Care and Education or equivalent.

Assistants should be qualified to NVQ II in Early Years Care and Education or equivalent.

The development of a high quality early years service is ongoing and the staff training needs should be evaluated regularly.

It is important for all staff to regularly update their knowledge in early years work.

NIPPA Training and Assessment Centre provides:

- An NVQ level II and III underpinning knowledge programme leading to a Certificate/Diploma in Early Years Practice.
- A range of modular training courses providing the underpinning knowledge to specific units of NVQ level II and III, allowing students to opt for those modules which best meet their training needs.
- A range of short courses and workshops which allows students to update their training.
- Assessment at levels II and III in Early Years Care and Education.

Information on these training courses and assessment is available from NIPPA central and regional offices. The NIPPA adviser will also be able to update creche staff with dates, times, cost and venues of courses in the locality.

Planning a One-Off Creche

The key to a successful creche is the amount of thought and preparation put in at the planning stage. One-off creches require just as much organisation as permanent creches

LEGAL REQUIREMENTS FOR OCCASIONAL DAY CARE FACILITIES

Article 121(4) Children (Northern Ireland) Order (1995) provides for day care facilities which are used on less than six days in a year to be exempt from the registration requirement. This exemption is intended to cover day care facilities set up for conferences and other occasional events. In all cases, before using the premises to provide day care for the first time, the organiser has to notify the relevant Trust that a day care facility is being provided. Information should be given about: the location, the numbers, age of the children, numbers of staff and opening hours. Where different organisations use the same premises, the six days apply in respect of each organisation not in respect of the premises. Guidance and Regulations Volume 2 (Para 6:23).

Planning for a one-off creche

Bring together all those who will be involved on the day. Prepare an action plan which includes consideration of the following questions:

Have the following been budgeted for?

- staff wages
- food for children's breaks and lunches
- transport of equipment
- travelling expenses for creche staff (if required)
- hire of room
- heat and electricity

Planning a One-Off Creche

CHECKLIST FOR A ONE-OFF CRECHE:

- How many children will be using the creche?
- Has a creche supervisor been appointed?
- Have staff been vetted by Social Services?
- How many staff will you need?
- What are the ages of the children?
- Have the premises been visited? Are they suitable and how many rooms will be available?
- Are the premises safe and hygienic? See checklist for creche premises and health and safety checklist
- What fee will be charged?
- How will equipment be transported to and from venue?
- Is there enough suitable equipment for the ages and stages of the children?
- Have the organisers of the event been informed of your requirements?
- Have the parents been informed of their role in preparing their child for the creche?
- Have staff met to discuss their role in organising the creche?
- How will children be settled into the creche?
- What action will be taken when a child will not settle?
- Who will be responsible for clearing away toys and equipment at the end of the session?
- Has a registration form been prepared as a means of collecting appropriate information about the child and whereabouts of the adults? See Appendix 1: Registration Form
- Has adequate insurance been obtained?
- Has a flexible routine been planned for the day to include children's need for food and drinks, rest and play?
- Who will do what?
- What equipment will be required?
- How will the play activities be presented?
- When will there be breaks?
- What routine will be provided?
- Who will welcome parents and children and keep the register?
- Where will the nappies be changed and how will soiled nappies be diposed of?
- Who will prepare the break/lunch?
- When will you meet to evaluate the day and learn from the experience for future events?

Play
Activities

Section 2

Play Activities

"Play is ACE!" *(Moyles 1994 p79)*

As wide a range of activities as possible should be provided. However, the range of activities on offer at any one time will be influenced by the size of the room, the age range of the children and the number of staff available. The following play activities should be provided:

- Play activities for babies
- Floor/table top play
- Imaginative play/home corner
- Junk play
- Music and rhymes
- Painting
- Physical play
- Playdough
- Sand play
- Storytelling
- Water play
- Alternative play

The following section looks at three aspects of each play activity:

1. Materials and equipment which will be needed for the play activity
2. Examples of what children are learning from these activities
3. The adults role in the activity

Creches often have a high turnover of staff and volunters. New staff have to learn appropriate skills quickly. They will need practical advice about their role in supervising the different play activities. This section may therefore be used as a tool for staff development. The different secctions may be copied and used as:

- Discussion tools during training sessions
- Induction handouts for new staff
- Posters which can be placed in different play areas outlining the adult's role
- Information to assist in evaluating existing practice

Play Activities for Babies

What You Will Need

- Blankets, floor cushions
- Colourful pictures, posters, photographs displayed low level
- Soft floor covering - carpeted area or piece of carpet which can be rolled up and put away if necessary
- Mobiles
- Activity centres
- Cuddly toys
- Noise making objects e.g. rattles, musical toys, bells, tins
- Colourful books containing pictures of everyday objects and photographs of people in familiar settings
- Stacking toys
- Posting boxes with different shapes
- Cardboard boxes for crawling in and out of
- Tins, boxes or baskets filled with natural objects for exploration
- Low level mirrors for babies to sit in front of
- Small mirrors which babies can hold
- Shape sorters
- Teething rings
- Soft blocks
- Hammer/peg boards
- Cradle gyms
- Telephones
- Tapes of songs and rhymes
- Push and pull along toys
- Activity mats
- Soft Play rings
- Toys should not be too small as babies could easily choke on them
- Make sure all toys are safe and non-toxic and meet the BSA safety regulations

Play Activities for Babies

What Babies Learn Through Play

- To explore the world through all of their senses
- To communicate through all of their senses
- To develop physical skills such as rolling, crawling, sitting, standing and walking
- To develop trust in other adults and children
- To imitate adults' expressions and movements
- To become aware of his/her own body's physical capabilities and limitations
- To watch people and learn from watching
- To practice making sounds
- To imitate sounds made by other people
- To be sociable and interact with other people outside of the family
- See also Alternative Play section on treasure baskets.

Play Activities for Babies

The Adult's Role

- To encourage communication skills through all the baby's senses: sight, sound, touch, taste, smell
- To hold the baby on the adult's knee for rocking, comfort and reassurance
- To use positive, warm, confident body language
- To use a soft, gentle tone of voice
- To sing or say rhymes which have lots of action in them
- To offer toys or rattles which make different sounds
- To offer a variety of play activities. Babies can make choices if given the opportunity
- To show babies colourful pictures, posters, photographs and talk about them
- To have lots of board books to show babies. Allow them to explore these with all of their senses
- To bring toys to babies - remember they cannot ask for what they want so they need to be able to see what is on offer
- To talk to babies, and name objects as you and the baby handle them
- To encourage physical activity i.e. sitting up, rolling, crawling, clapping hands, waving arms, reaching out, grasping
- To ensure all toys are safe and non-toxic
- To ensure all items are clean. Toys that go in a babies mouth should be cleaned before giving them to another child.
- To make sounds and stimulate acquisition of language through talking and cooing etc.
- To imitate sounds that the baby makes.
- To place babies in different positions. For example, place them on their stomach so they can practise lifting their heads and rolling over.
- To let babies fill containers with objects and tip them out.
- To play peek-a-boo or other games in which you disappear and reappear.

Adults need to be responsive to the changing needs of babies. Babies need to be cared for by one adult whom they can get to know. It is particularly important in a creche for staff to decide who will be caring for the babies.

Floor/Table Play

What You Will Need

- Child-sized tables and chairs
- Soft floor covering, carpet, car mats, road mats
- Zoo and zoo animals
- Farm and farm animals
- Doll's house and people
- Garage and cars
- Jigsaws
- Duplo
- Building blocks-preferably wooden
- Construction toys
- Threading activities
- Lotto and matching games
- Mark making materials-pens, crayons, pencils, paper
- Catalogues, cards for cutting and pasting
- Storage boxes

What are Children Learning

- To use their imagination and creativity
- To develop language skills and to talk about what they are doing
- To put together and take apart
- To balance and manipulate equipment
- To build, construct and design
- To plan and make choices
- To identify shapes and match them with similar ones
- To share with others
- To build towers and knock them down - cause and effect
- To develop mathematical skills e.g. counting, sorting, matching, one to one correspondence.

Floor/Table Play

The Adult's Role

- To ensure that there are enough materials for each child
- To make materials accessible to children
- To observe children playing and look out for opportunities to extend the play by introducing different materials
- To get down to the children's level when joining in with their play
- To talk with children about what they are doing. Describe what you see. Describe what they are doing eg. "you are putting one block on top of another", "it's high" or "it's small"
- Try not to assume what the child is thinking
- To encourage children to put toys back into the boxes from which they were taken
- To ensure that toys do not block passage ways
- To display a variety of table top toys and allow the children to choose for themselves
- To ask children open questions: How? What? When? Where?
- To offer encouragement to the children

Floor play is particularly suitable for younger children. Many of the materials listed could be played with on the floor. Always be aware of safety issues around the size of beads as small items could be easily swallowed or cause choking.

Imaginative Play/Home Corner

What You Will Need

- Small furniture e.g. fridge, cooker, sink unit, tables, chairs (preferably wooden)
- Home corner dividers
- Lots of dressing up clothes with velcro or other easy fastenings
- Hats and shoes
- Lengths of material, pieces of lace, curtains etc.
- Bags and baskets
- Cardboard boxes, shoe boxes
- Shoes, jewellery, spectacles
- Variety of pots and pans
- Scales, cooking utensils
- Tablecloths
- Iron and ironing board, brush and dustpan
- Variety of dolls, reflecting gender, race and disability; soft toys, babywear and accessories
- Household items e.g. clocks, ornaments, telephones and directories, plants - plastic and real
- Clearly identified prop boxes for specific role play e.g. hairdresser, baby shop, grocer, travel agent, castle, den, post office, fire station, library
- Lots of natural and real materials which encourage young children to talk about their experiences

What Children are Learning

- To develop an understanding of a variety of roles e.g. mum, dad, baby, doctor, nurse, shopkeeper etc.
- To develop language for everyday living
- To develop imagination and creativity
- To solve problems
- To co-ordinate and manipulate materials
- To develop mathematical skills: matching, sorting, sequencing
- To experience a sense of control of the environment
- To explore through fantasy play, emotions felt in their life's experience
- To make decisions and carry through an idea to a conclusion
- To share and co-operate with others

Children benefit greatly from having the opportunity to play with real items. Parents can be encouraged to bring items such as clothes, shoes, jewellery and kitchen utensils from home. Listen to the children's role play and respond to their imaginations in order to extend and develop their play environment.

Imaginative Play/Home Corner

The Adult's Role

- To enter into the spirit of the child's imagination
- To observe the children's play at first and then, if appropriate, join in
- To talk to children in a conversational style: e.g. "I'm going on holiday soon" or "A funny thing happened to me today at the shops"
- To introduce more materials when an appropriate opportunity arises
- To ask open questions which will extend the fantasy play: i.e. How? What? When? Where?
- To encourage children to tidy up when they are finished playing
- To listen carefully and, if appropriate, encourage a positive attitude to other children
- To ensure materials are clean and well maintained

Junk Play

What You Will Need

- Child-sized tables and chairs or clear floor space
- Any empty, clean household junk
- Containers, boxes, paper bags, packaging, large bottle tops, egg boxes and cardboard tubes
- Natural materials, pine cones, pasta, shells, leaves, feathers and fabrics of varying textures
- Scissors, brushes, spatulas, paint, etc.
- Joiners such as P.V.A., cellotape, string, Pritt stick, Copydex (non-toxic)
- Cleaning materials and a bin for waste

What Children are Learning

- Knowledge of the properties of various materials
- To develop self expression
- To design and make constructions of their choice
- To solve problems
- To co-operate and share with each other
- One to one matching
- The different ways in which materials can be joined
- To notice sameness and difference
- To make choices and follow through on personal thoughts and ideas
- To be creative
- To relax and enjoy working with different materials

The Adult's Role

- To provide the materials
- To have a good supply of junk materials, scissors and glue on offer
- To separate materials out into categories. Use shoe boxes, cardboard boxes, margarine tubs etc. for presenting materials
- To help children to master skills such as cutting and sticking
- To observe how children use the materials
- To encourage children to experiment and solve problems
- To make choosing materials fun
- To allow children to make their own choices
- To introduce new materials and describe them
- To have conversations with children rather than giving directions
- To be aware that children do not need to make anything at all. Just 'doing' is fun
- To encourage children to talk about what they are doing
- To ask open questions: How? What? Where? When?
- To observe children's concentration and comment on this e.g. "I see you are working really hard"
- To help children to develop the language to talk about what they are doing
- To be patient and supportive

Music and Sound

What You Will Need

- Rattles
- Chimes
- Squeakers
- A range of musical instruments e.g. whistles, triangles, blocks, castanets, shakers, maracas, chimebars
- Homemade instruments e.g. drums made out of boxes or shakers out of plastic pots
- Tapes of familiar sounds and of different styles of music such as classical, opera, jazz, rock
- Tape Recorder
- A collection of songbooks
- Your voice!

N.B. Do not have the radio or background tapes on throughout the session

What Children are Learning

- To listen
- To imitate other children and adults
- To develop their voices
- To make sounds for themselves
- To move in rhythm to music and sounds
- To gain self confidence and self expression
- To develop language which describes sounds, movements and pitch
- To develop an awareness of rhyming sounds
- To develop pitch
- To become confident in expressing themselves vocally
- To sing and enjoy music

Music and Sound

The Adult's Role

- To bring children together for group activities
- To sing songs with children
- To use music in a group or one to one situations rather than as a background noise
- To encourage children to sing and use their voices
- To build up a repertoire of songs and rhymes both old and new
- To use songs/music from different cultures
- To introduce instruments to children
- To allow children to select instruments of their own choosing
- To give children the words to describe the instruments
- To give children the words to describe the sounds they hear and the types of music
- To encourage children to relax and enjoy the pleasure of music and sound
- To have fun

Painting

What You Will Need

- Child-sized tables or painting easels
- Various sizes of paint brushes - thick handled brushes are easier for very young children to manipulate
- Large pieces of paper: newsprint, wallpaper, computer paper
- Non spill paint pots
- Liquid or powder paint
- Protection for children's clothes. An old shirt, apron or waterproof overalls are ideal
- Covering for the floor and tables
- Protection for adult's clothes
- Somewhere to dry the paintings e.g. plastic clothes drier or table
- Basin or sink to wash hands and individual or paper towels
- Other materials to extend the experience and creativity eg. sponges, printing materials, etc.

What Children are Learning

- To discover the pleasures of colour and how to control paint in order to create the designed result
- To plan and design
- To develop self expression
- To experiment with different shades, tones and materials
- To experiment with up and down and round and round strokes, dots and dashes, filling the whole page
- To hold the paint brush to control an end result
- To put on an overall
- To use language to describe what they are thinking and feeling
- To construct stories and images in the mind about what they are painting
- To choose materials themselves and develop a sense of independance
- To distinguish between wet and dry
- To relax and enjoy the therapeutic nature of painting

The Adult's Role

- To supervise the children
- To help children to put on and take off and hang up overalls
- To help children to wash and dry hands
- To hang up paintings to dry
- To help children make choices
- To make sure children have enough paper, paint, brushes etc.
- To put the child's name on his/her work, preferably on the back of their painting
- To encourage children to explore and experiment
- To reinforce the few rules in a positive manner:
    "keep paint in the painting area"
    "put on an overall"
- To talk to the children about their work
- To talk about the colours, the shapes, the materials
- To describe what children are doing
- To ask open questions: How? When? What? Where?
- To hold back from asking "What is it?" or "Is it a ....?"

Remember the adult's idea of how a painting should look can often stifle the child's own creativity and pleasure in the activity.

Physical Play

What You Will Need

- Sit and push toys suitable for toddlers
- Small trikes for older children learning to pedal
- Push along toys which help with learning to walk
- Tumble mats or a well carpeted area
- Small slide and climbing frame
- Safety mats
- Cardboard boxes for climbing in and out of
- Songs, rhymes and games which allow lots of large muscle movement
- Outdoor play space
- See Saw
- Tunnels
- Hula Hoops and bean bags

What Children are Learning

- To use self expression and develop self confidence and independence
- To co-operate with others and follow simple safety rules eg. "no pushing"
- To follow the rules of games and codes of behaviour
- To solve problems and explore the environment with their bodies
- To understand force, distance, height and gradient
- To develop co-ordination and fine and gross motor movement
- To engage in challenging activities
- To improve balance and develop physical skills such as crawling, walking, lifting, pulling, pushing, rolling, climbing, stretching, rocking, clapping and sliding

The Adult's Role

- To supervise and inspect the equipment for safety
- To set boundaries e.g. 'no pushing on slide'
- To encourage children to explore, climb, pedal, push etc.
- To ask open questions: How? Why? When? Where?
- To positively encourage appropriate active behaviour by use of language and imitation
- To model physical behaviour through rhymes, movement and games
- To observe children's play and join in activities when appropriate
- To provide support and encouragement for all children

Playdough

What You Will Need

- Child-sized tables and chairs
- Sufficient quantity of dough for each child -
    coloured/plain
    textured
    elastic and non elastic dough
    for recipes - see Appendix 7
- Airtight storage containers
- Rollers
- Pattern makers
- Flour
- Flour shaker
- Scales
- Aprons
- Cutters - animals, shapes etc.
- Real baking tins
- Plates
- Basin or sink to wash hands in and paper towels to dry them

What Children are Learning

- To manipulate, roll, flatten and shape
- To make comparisons
- To explore materials
- To develop all of their senses
- To develop language and vocabulary
- To develop imagination
- To realize that it is alright to get your hands messy - a good lesson for life!
- To express emotions. Playdough can be squeezed and thumped. It can be a great way of diffusing anger and frustation
- To make playdough
- To enjoy the therapeutic nature of playdough

The Adult's Role

- To sit with the children at a table
- To allow the children to explore the dough
- To make sure that there is enough dough for each child
- To renew dough regularly as it gets dirty when so many children are playing with it
- To observe the children and listen to what they are saying
- To talk to the child in a conversational style and reinforce learning as appropriate
- To ask open questions: What? Why? When? How?
- To comment on what children are doing rather than telling them what to do
- To introduce tools to play only when it is observed that the children have exhausted playing with the dough on its own
- To assist children to wash and dry their hands after playing with the dough
- To encourage the children to tidy up after playing with the dough

Sand Play

What You Will Need

- Sand tray
- Silver sand
- Sand wheel
- Small buckets and containers
- Sieves and colanders
- Scales
- Funnels and bottles
- Set of measuring spoons
- Small plastic plant pots
- Flour scoops
- Materials to extend imaginative play eg. pebbles, shells, twigs and leaves
- Storage shelves, vegetable racks or baskets to display toys for children to choose
- Dustpan and brush - children enjoy helping to sweep up spilled sand

What Children are Learning

- To explore the nature and properties of dry and wet sand
- To develop investigative skills e.g. the different properties of sand
- To make patterns in the sand with shapes, hands and buckets
- To fill and empty containers
- To develop mathematical skills of volume, amount, weight
- To develop control of large and small muscles
- To develop use of language and growth of imagination
- To relax and enjoy the therapeutic nature of sand

The Adult's Role

- To ensure sand is clean and the tray is adequately filled
- To stay close by the area, supervise closely and observe children's play
- To make sure the toys and equipment are clearly displayed
- To ensure the floor is covered and spills are brushed up regularly
- To encourage sharing and taking turns
- To talk to children about what they are doing, e.g. "You're pouring sand and making the wheel turn round", using a conversational style rather than questioning or giving directions
- To encourage children to explore and experiment
- To positively reinforce the guidelines for managing the play e.g. "It's dangerous to throw sand"
- To replace the sand on a regular basis

Storytelling

What You Will Need

- Suitable storage: bookcase or rack
- A wide variety of board books
- Finger play and action rhyme books
- Books with moving parts
- Books reflecting real life situations: real people doing ordinary, everyday things
- Books which show men in traditional women's roles and women in traditional men's roles
- Books which reflect our multicultural society and celebrate our differences and our similarities
- Props for storytelling without books i.e. puppets, pictures, prop bag filled with different items such as cars, teapots, jewellery etc.
- Comfortable seats, cushions or beanbags. Young children like to get down on the floor and look at books, or curl up on a cushion or chair. Creating this environment helps them to feel at home in the creche and to accept reading as a pleasurable activity

What The Child Is Learning

- To make choices about what they like to read
- To see how a book works i.e. to turn pages from right to left and to know which is the front and which is the back
- To understand that a story has a beginning, a middle and an end
- To understand that words carry meaning
- To learn new words
- To build up a knowledge of favourite stories
- To catch the "reading bug": much of the skill and pleasure of reading is caught not taught
- To express emotions and feelings through the written word

The Adult's Role

- To read to children when they want to be read to
- To observe quietly for a few minutes - children may already be happily looking at the books and putting their own words to the stories. If they are, then let them continue to do this
- To encourage children to choose books
- To be enthusiastic. Your tone of voice is vital to the enjoyment of the story
- To tell a story without a book. Children will love to watch your facial expressions and join in with improvised sounds and movements. Some of the traditional nursery stories lend themselves to this well.
- To hold babies on the adult's lap, showing them books and talking about the pictures
- To encourage children to respect books and look after them
- To remove dirty and torn books
- To allow children to get up and leave during a story. Young children have a shorter attention span than adults and forcing them to sit when they have lost interest is counter-productive

Water Play

What You Will Need

- Protective overalls which prevent children's feet and sleeves from getting wet
- Water wheel and pumps
- Small medium and large sized containers
- Plastic bottles with holes at different levels
- Plastic tubing of different lengths
- Things that float - corks, ping-pong balls etc.
- Things that sink - stones etc.
- Funnels of different sizes
- Small metal teapot with hinged lid
- Metal watering can with thin spout
- Small buckets and bowls
- Boats
- Water and sea animals
- Storage shelves, vegetable racks or baskets to display toys for children to choose
- Materials for mopping up spilt water

What Children are Learning

- To explore the nature and properties of water and other liquids
- To control the flow of water by blowing down tubes or pouring through different containers
- To experiment with things that float and sink
- To co-ordinate hand and eye skills - pouring from one container to another is a skilled operation
- To use language to describe what they see and what is happening eg. full, empty, small, large, wet, dry, sink, float etc.
- To make discoveries about volume and capacity
- To relax and enjoy the therapeutic nature of water

The Adult's Role

- To have realistic expectations of how children at different stages will use water
- To encourage children to put on an overall and roll up sleeves
- To ensure the water is clean and the tray is adequately filled
- To ensure the water is lukewarm throughout the play time
- To stay close by the area, supervise closely and observe children's play. If toddlers are playing with the water the adult will need to sit at the water tray with them
- To ensure that toys and equipment are clearly displayed
- To mop up spills regularly. Children will enjoy helping with this task
- To talk to the children about what they are doing, using a conversational style
- To ask questions sparingly
- To encourage children to explore and experiment
- To remove items from the water perodically so that the tray does not become overcrowded
- To have paper towels ready and accessible for drying hands

Alternative Play

Treasure Baskets - Babies 6-9 months approximately

Babies need a wide variety of objects, both bought and natural, to engage their interest and stimulate their developing senses and understanding.

Elinor Goldschmied (1994) developed the concept of 'Treasure baskets'. Babies - never more than three at a time-are positioned around a low, flat-bottemed basket with no handle. The basket is filled to the brim with a range of natural objects to stimulate the babies' senses of touch, smell, taste, sound and sight. Babies are free to sort through and select what appeals to them. By sucking, mouthing and handling the objects, they are finding out about weight, size, shapes, texture, sound and smell. During this play it is the adult's role to provide the security of an attentive but not active presence.

Heuristic Play - Children 12-20 months

Heuristic play allows for very young children to explore a range of everyday objects and containers by themselves and for themselves without active adult intervention.

The video, "Infants at Work", shows infants engaged in Treasure basket play.

The video, "Heuristic Play with Objects", shows children engaged in Heuristic play.

The NIPPA course - 0-2's Workshops - Alternative Play examines providing Treasure Basket play and Heurisitic play in early years settings.

Child Management

Section 3

Child Management

Managing Children's Behaviour

All creches should have an agreed policy on how they will respond to children's behaviour. This policy needs to be shared with staff and parents and should be an integral part of the induction process for new staff. A shared approach to child management will ensure children know what to expect. They feel secure in an atmosphere of shared responsibility.

NIPPA believes in young children's growing ability to control their own lives, to make choices and accept responsibility for their actions. NIPPA also believes that all children have the right to expect positive approaches to discipline which are consistent with these goals.

Try to create a welcoming positive atmosphere. When the children come through the door for the first time they are naturally anxious and fearful. This is not a surprising reaction when we look at what we are asking from them:

- To accept and trust adults whom they have never met
- To make friends with new children
- To stay with adults and children they do not know
- To feel at home and comfortable in a new place
- To play freely with equipment and toys they have never seen

As adults when we visit someone's home for the first time it is natural to feel slightly uncomfortable:

- We are unsure of the other person's rules
- We don't know where to go to the toilet
- We don't know where to go to get a drink
- Do we take off our shoes?
- Do we hang up our coat etc?

Adults must be sensitive to the natural anxieties some children may experience when they stay in a creche for the first time.

Confusion, lack of understanding and fear are factors which can adversely affect children's behaviour. When creche staff are planning their provision it might be helpful to discuss the above points to be able to empathise with how the children might be feeling.

For information on creating a welcoming atmosphere see:-
Appendix 5: Settling Children into the Creche, an Information Sheet for Creche Staff.

Smacking or any punishment that humilates, attacks children's sense of self and makes them feel helpless is damaging and should never be permitted.

Further information on managing children's behaviour can be found in the NIPPA publication: Discipline/Child Management in Early Years Settings.

Developing a Child Management Policy

- Approach children at their physical level and make eye contact sensitively
- Speak to the children in a quiet assertive tone of voice
- Cut out long waiting periods such as at snack time or trips to the toilet. Allow children to be involved in preparing and serving snacks
- Set clear boundaries but keep rules to the minimum
- Give clear consistent explanations for these rules. For example "Walk in the creche. There isn't enough room to run"
- Agree on expectations and rules and remain consistent in following them through. If something is unacceptable today, it is unacceptable tomorrow
- Take time to listen to and involve children's ideas and points of view
- Let the children see that you are a team and are happy to work together. This is shown by exchange of comments, looks and smiles
- Accept that children are functioning at different levels of development and understanding. One of these stages is a natural fear of strangers
- Use positive comments to guide children's behaviour. Constant "nos" and "don'ts" create a very negative atmosphere
- Recognise and respond to acceptable behaviour with praise and encouragement
- Be specific when encouraging children. Describe what they are doing. For example "I see you are working very hard today building the blocks"
- Avoid labelling children especially as "naughty" or "bad". Labels can create a very negative self image and can lead to scapegoating.

Appendices

Appendix 1

CRECHE: _____

Sample Registration Form

Child's Full Name: _____
(Please underline name by which child is known)

Address: _____

Age: _____ Date of Birth: _____

Where can we find you during the session? e.g. Which class? What room?

_____

Child's Doctor: _____

Address: _____

Telephone Number: _____

Health (allergies, illness, etc): _____

Special dietary requirements: _____

Toilet (nappy, potty, toilet): _____

Put any special word the child uses for 'toilet' or 'comforter': _____

When, and for how long, does your child sleep during the day? _____

Anything else you feel we should know about your child? _____

If possible, please bring along a change of clothes, nappies, cotton wool and creams (if required) made-up bottles or spoon feeds. These items should be brought in a clearly labelled bag.

If your child is suffering from an infectious disease, or is obviously 'unwell', we would ask that they remain at home.

SAMPLE ADMINISTRATION OF MEDICINE

CHILD'S NAME: _____

ADDRESS: _____

_____

FAMILY DOCTOR: _____

DOSAGE REQUIRED: _____

TIME DOSAGE TO BE GIVEN: _____

NUMBER OF DAYS DOSAGE REQUIRED: _____

NB - Please notify staff of any dosage given before coming to creche

Would you please ensure that my child is given the medicine according to the above instructions. I hereby authorise.

_____ to give the medicine or in her absence a delegated person.

SIGNED: _____ **(PARENT)**

DATE: _____

SIGNED: _____ **(G.P.)**

DATE: _____

DOSAGE GIVEN	BY WHOM	DATE / TIME

Appendix 3

SAMPLE INFORMATION ON ILLNESSES

Information to parents and carers on illness. Please keep for reference.

CRECHE: _____

Our creche looks after children in a wide age range. Young children are particularly susceptible to infections. In order to protect your child, and others, we ask you not to bring them to the creche if they are unwell.

As vomiting and diarrhoea (with or without a specified diagnosis) may be particularly infectious we ask you not to bring your child to the creche until the diarrhoea and vomiting has settled for a period of at least 24 hours.

Childhood Illnesses

The following is a list of common childhood illnesses and the minimum recommended length of time for which the child should not attend the creche:

Gastro-enteritis	-	At least 48 hours after symptoms have stopped
Chickenpox	-	14 days from start of rash/until scabs are dry
Measles	-	10 days from start of rash
Rubella	-	7 days from start of rash
Whooping cough	-	28 days from start of cough
Mumps	-	7 days from when the swelling subsides
Conjunctivitis	-	14 days from start of infection
Scabies	-	Until adequate treatment administered
Impetigo	-	Until recovered and free from symptoms

CRECHE THANKS YOU FOR YOUR CO-OPERATION
IN PROTECTING YOUR CHILD AND OTHERS

SETTLING YOUR CHILD INTO THE CRECHE - SAMPLE INFORMATION SHEET

Tips for Parents

For most parents leaving your child in a group setting for the first time can be an anxious experience. However these few tips may help ease the process and make it a pleasant time for both parent and child. Remember an anxious parent may lead to an anxious child.

1. Before the first visit talk casually and positively to your child about the setting.
    Play games and read books and stories relating to this experience.

2. Before attending the setting, leave your child for short periods with granny, auntie, or a relative. Make sure your child knows you will be back. This way they get used to your absence and enjoy the happy reunion.

3. On the first visit, stay with your child while they meet staff and explore equipment for the first time. This helps your child to see the setting as an extension of the home expereince as opposed to a frightening break from it.

4. On the first day, and maybe for the first few days, leave your child in the group for short periods. This may be awkward for you but putting the effort in at this crucial settling-in time will have its rewards in enabling your child to stay happily without you. Be guided by the staff and your child's key worker. Remember they have seen it all before and are experienced in helping your child feel happy.

5. On the first day don't just disappear. Tell your child when and where you are going, and that you will be back soon.

6. Show your child clearly that you are on good terms with staff. This helps your child to feel secure.

7. If your child asks you to stay with him/her, say "yes". Don't say, "parents aren't allowed into the group". You will be encouraged to stay until your child is happy and settled.

8. If your child has a favourite toy, bring it with him. It may help him/her to feel safe. Make sure the staff know about this. It is probably best to put your child's name on the toy.

These tips have been tried and tested and shown to help. There is no perfect formula. Whatever works for you and your child is the best approach.

Appendix 5

SETTLING CHILDREN INTO THE CRECHE - SAMPLE INSTRUCTION SHEET

Tips for Staff

The First Days and Before

1. Settling in doesn't begin on the day a child starts the creche. The planning and preparation prior to this day is what counts. **FIRST IMPRESSIONS LAST.**

2. Make the parent and child feel genuinely welcome. Take time to chat to the parent in a friendly manner.

3. Give the parent a leaflet or hand-out with information about your creche before the first day if possible.

4. Hold an Open Day.

5. Talk to the parents about what they can do to prepare their child for the creche. See Appendix 4: "Tips for Parents".

6. Take time to talk to the child. Get down to their level and make sensitive eye contact.

7. Encourage parents to stay with their child until settled. They should not simply disappear. The child should be told when and where the parent is going and that they will be back. Parents might like to leave something to show they will be returning.

8. Take the parent and child on a tour of the room and describe the activities available.

9. Familiarise the parent and child with the names of the different areas of play.

10. Introduce the parent to other members of staff.

11. Introduce the children to each other, not too many at first. Follow the child's lead.

12. The first stay should be for a short period. Parents should come back quickly. This will enable the children to trust the staff when they say mummy/daddy will be back soon. Gradually the child will feel safe and happy to stay for longer periods.

13. Children should not be left to cry for long periods of time. Parents should be informed that they will be called back to the creche if their child does not settle.

SAMPLE CONTRACT BETWEEN CRECHE AND PARENT/CARER

CRECHE: _____

I, the parent/carer of _____ , agree to comply with the following conditions:

1. I will assist in the settling of my child.

2. If my child does not settle, I will be asked to return to the creche.

3. My child will be looked after only during the agreed time period.

4. Should I no longer require a creche place for my child, I will inform the supervisor so that another child may be given the place.

5. I will tell staff if anyone other than myself is collecting my child.

6. I agree that nobody under the age of 16 years will collect my child.

7. If my child is absent from the creche for more than 2 weeks without explanation it will be assumed I no longer require a place.

Signed: _____ Parent/Carer

Date: _____

Appendix 7

DOUGH RECIPES

Basic Dough
3 cups plain flour

1 cup salt

water to mix, with a little food colouring added

Mix all together to a pastry consistency

Keep in an airtight container

Modelling Dough
2 cups plain flour

2 cups salt

2 tbsps wallpaper paste (non-fungicidal)

1 cup water

Mix ingredients together and knead until smooth.

Make shapes and models and allow them to harden overnight or

bake in the oven-200°F or 100°C for 3-4 hours.

Boiled Dough
4 cups plain flour

2 cups salt

8 teaspoons cream of tartar

4 cups water - food colouring added to water

1/2 cup cooking oil

Mix ingredients in a saucepan and stir over medium

heat until mixture thickens and combines into one lump

Tip onto pastry board and when cool, knead until smooth.

Keeps well in an airtight container.

Replace frequently.

NIPPA PUBLICATIONS

- Accounts Book
- Child Observation and Recording: Curriculum Planning and Evaluation
- Choosing Childcare and Education
- Code of Practice for Parent and Toddler Groups
- Equal Opportunities Policy Statement for Groups
- Guidelines for Setting up and Implementing a Complaints Procedure
- Healthy Eating Policy for Pre-Schoool Children
- I Want to Play
- Parent and Toddler Register
- Playgroup Register
- Protecting Children: Principles and Practice Guidelines for Early Years Workers
- Recruitment and Selection Guidelines for the Employment of Early Years Staff
- The Effective Committee
- Valuing Play, Valuing Early Childhood: Policy and Practice Guidleines for Early Years Practitioners
- Working with Parents: An Information Pack for Early Years Settings

P.L.A.

Learning in Pre-School: Planning a Curriculum for the Under Fives

Play Activities Series:
- Books and Stories
- Clay and Dough
- Glueing
- Make Believe
- Paint and Print
- Sand and Water
- Wood

Running a Parent & Toddler Group

Further Reading

Abbot L and Moylett H. (1997) 'Working with the Under-Threes': *Training and Professional Developments'* Bristol. Open University Press

Andreski R & Nicholls S. (1996) 'Managing Your Nursery *- A Practical Guide for Nursery Professionals'* London. Nursery World

Sadek E & Sadek J. (1996) 'Good Practice in Nursery Management' Cheltenham. Stanley Thornes

Beaver M, Brewster J, Jones P, Keene A, Neaum S, Tallack J. (1994) 'Babies and Young Children Book I *- Development 0-7'* London. Stanley Thornes

Birch C and Houghton N. (1990) 'The ABC of Creche Training' London. The Daycare Trust

Donoghue J. (1998) 'Running a Mother and Toddler Club' London. George Allen and Unwin

Goldschmied E. & Jackson S. (1994) 'People Under Three - Young Children in Daycare' London. Routledge

Green C. Dr. (1992) 'Toddler Taming - A Parents Guide to the First Four Years' London. Vermillion

Melhurst E.C. & Moss P. (1991) 'Daycare for young Children - International Perspectivis' London. Routledge

Whalley Margy (1994), 'Learning to be Strong, Settling up a Neighbourhood Service for Under-Fives and their Families' Great Britain. Hodder and Stoughton.

Moyles Janet R. (1994) 'The Excellence of Play' Buckingham. Open University Press.

Pace M. (1999) 'Starting a Nursery - A Practical Guide for Early Years Professionals' London. Nursery World

Social Services Offices

SOCIAL SERVICES OFFICES

EASTERN HEALTH AND SOCIAL SERVICES BOARD

S & E BELFAST HEALTH & SOCIAL SERVICES TRUST
Glen Villa, Knockbracken Health Care Park
Saintfield Road, BELFAST BT8 8BH
Tel: 028 9056 4911

DOWN & LISBURN HEALTH & SOCIAL SERVICES
TRUST
Warren House, Children's Resource Centre
61 Woodland Park, LISBURN BT28 ILQ
Tel: 028 9260 7528   Fax: 028 9260 7541

ULSTER COMMUNITY HEALTH AND SOCIAL
SERVICES TRUST
Dunlop Units, Units 57 & 58, 4 Balloo Drive
BANGOR BTI9 7QY
Tel: 028 9127 0672

N & W BELFAST HEALTH & SOCIAL SERVICES TRUST
16 Cupar Street, BELFAST BTI3 2LJ
Tel: 028 9032 0840

DOWN & LISBURN HEALTH & SOCIAL SERVICES
TRUST
81 Market Street, DOWNPATRICK BT30 6LZ
Tel: 028 4461 3511   Fax: 028 4461 5994

NORTHERN HEALTH AND SOCIAL SERVICES BOARD

HOMEFIRST COMMUNITY TRUST
Childcare Services, Ellis Street Complex
CARRICKFERGUS BT38 8AZ
Tel: 028 9335 1424

HOMEFIRST COMMUNITY TRUST
Audley Terrace, 27 Ballymoney Road
BALLYMENA BT43 5BS
Tel: 028 2561 1207

CAUSEWAY TRUST
Riverside House, Portstewart Road, COLERAINE
Tel: 028 7035 8158

HOMEFIRST COMMUNITY TRUST
Sperrin House, 43 Queen Avenue
MAGHERAFELT BT45 6BX
Tel: 028 7930 1700

HOMEFIRST COMMUNITY TRUST
Fieldwork Office, 52 Orritor Road
COOKSTOWN BT80 8BN
Tel: 028 8676 2762

WESTERN HEALTH AND SOCIAL SERVICES BOARD

FOYLE COMMUNITY TRUST
Birch villa, Gransha Park
Clooney Road, LONDONDERRY BT47 ITF
Tel: 028 7186 5126

SPERRIN LAKELAND HEALTH & SOCIAL
CARE TRUST
Hospital & Community Services Unit
Tyrone & Fermanagh Hospital
OMAGH BT79 ONS
Tel:- 028 8224 3232

SPERRIN LAKELAND HEALTH & SOCIAL CARE TRUST
Enniskillen Community Services, 2 Coleshill Road
ENNISKILLEN BT74 7HG
Tel: 028 6634 4000

SOUTHERN HEALTH AND SOCIAL SERVICES BOARD

NEWRY & MOURNE HEALTH & SOCIAL SERVICES
TRUST
John Mitchell Place, NEWRY BT34 2BP
Tel: 028 3026 7030

CRAIGAVON & BANBRIDGE COMMUNITY HEALTH &
SOCIAL SERVICES TRUST
Lurgan Health & Social Services Centre
100 Sloan Street, LURGAN BT66 8NT
Tel: 028 2832 7824

CRAIGAVON & BANBRIDGE COMMUNITY HEALTH &
SOCIAL SERVICES TRUST
Brownlow Health & Social Services Centre
I Legahory Centre, Legahory
CRAIGAVON BT65 SBE
Tel: 028 3834 3011

ARMAGH & DUNGANNON TRUST
Gosford Place, The Mall, ARMAGH BT61 9AR
Tel: 028 3752 2262

CRAIGAVON & BANBRIDGE COMMUNITY HEALTH &
SOCIAL SERVICES TRUST
Banbridge Health & Social Services Centre
Scarva Street, BANBRIDGE
Tel: 028 4066 2866

CRAIGAVON & BANBRIDGE COMMUNITY HEALTH &
SOCIAL SERVICES TRUST
Health & Social Services Centre
Tavanagh Avenue, Portadown, CRAIGAVON BT62 3BU
Tel: 028 3835 1177